LADDERS

Youngest player opens the game—and throws any number to start. If your counter lands on the foot of a ladder you climb it—but if it lands on head of spook down you go to the tail. First player to end exactly on 100 wins.

95	94	93	92	91
86	87	88		90
75	74	73	72	71
66	67	68		
55		53	52	51
46		48	49	50
35	34	33	32	31
26	27	28	29	30
15		13	12	11
6	7	8	9	10

D1337193

3

95p

WEBSTER

HORRORNATION STREET

8

DEMON DiFFereNces

These pictures of the scaries of Scream Inn look alike, but our fiendish artist has made 10 small alterations to the lower one. Can you spot them?

ANSWERS: 1. Support missing under window; 2. Larger skull on sign; 3. Pair of eyes in doorway; 4. Pattern on witch's handkerchief; 5. Spider hanging from window; 6. Chain missing from Suffering Sam's leg; 7. Larger moon; 8. Bertie Bedsheet has a hunched shoulder; 9. Man has larger beret; 10. More whiskers on man.

The HAND

PHEW — FINISHED! NOW TO COLLECT THE MONEY THE MAN PROMISED ME FOR CLEARING THE SNOW OFF HIS PATH!

HOP IT! I'LL PRETEND I DID THE WORK AND COLLECT THE CASH!

THAT SNEAKY BULLY'S NOT GETTING AWAY WITH THAT!

OUCH! ROTTER!

COOEE! SIR — THE SNOW'S CLEARED!

SWEEP!

SWOOSH!

THIS WILL MAKE HIS PLAN GO "ADRIFT"!

WHO ARE YOU TRYING TO DIDDLE? CLEAR ALL THAT OFF BEFORE YOU GET PAID!

HUH?

BAH! CATCH ME CLEARING ANY SNOW!

SIGH! I'LL HAVE TO START ALL OVER AGAIN WHEN HE'S GONE!

I'LL HELP HIM!

11

GRIMLY FEENDISH

AH! IT'S WIMBLEDON FORTNIGHT! A GREAT OPPORTUNITY TO STEAL LOTS OF LOOT!

TENNIS AT WIMBLEDON

HEH, HEH! MY FIRST VICTIMS — ENGROSSED IN WATCHING THE TENNIS, AS I EXPECTED!

WE'LL HELP OURSELVES TO THE SILVER AND OTHER VALUABLES!

H'MM! QUITE A LOT OF MONEY IN THIS BLOKE'S POCKETS!

A NICE GOLD WATCH HERE, MR. FEENDISH!

WOULD YOU GET UP, SIR, WHILE I STEAL YOUR SETTEE?

THAT'S THE LOT, MR. FEENDISH!

GOOD! TAKE YOUR TIME, SQUELCH, THERE'S NO RUSH!

16

EEK! NOW THE HOUSE IS BACK TO NORMAL!

WHOOSH!

JUST A MINUTE! THAT MEANS...

OH, NO!

WHUPPP!

SHRIEK!

WHERE AM I?

AH—I REMEMBER NOW!

WHAM!

GMMPH!

AS I WAS SAYING, THANKS FOR CATCHING ME, DAD— I COULD HAVE HURT MYSELF!

GROAN! 'SHRINK' NOTHING OF IT, SON!

Ghouldilocks

EEK! MY WASHING!

COO! THAT NAUGHTY MAN'S PINCHING CLOTHES OFF THE LINE!

WOW! HE'S A RAG MAN! I'LL NIP AHEAD AND TEACH HIM A LESSON!

OLD RAGS BOUGHT & SOLD

IN ANOTHER GARDEN...

CLIP-CLOP! CLIP-CLOP!

HERE HE COMES, I'D BETTER GET READY!

HEH, HEH! I'LL GET A GOOD HAUL HERE!

YERK! WHO SAID THAT?

OY! STOP THAT!

YAAGH!

BOP!

I DID!

The Duke's Spook

21

SOMETHING UNFORESEEN IS ALWAYS HAPPENING WHEN HE'S AROUND! —

WIZARD PRANG *in* **DEMON DRUID** — HE SPELLS TROUBLE FOR JUST ABOUT EVERYONE!

Wiz War!

I'D BETTER TAKE A CRAFTY PEEP IN ME CRYSTAL BALL TO SEE IF ANYTHING GOOD IS GOING TO HAPPEN TO ME TODAY!

GOOD THINGS — BAD THINGS

OH, WOE IS ME! NOTHING GOOD IS GOING TO HAPPEN TO ME TODAY!

GOOD THINGS

DARE I LOOK INTO THE BAD BALL TO SEE WHAT LIES IN STORE?

I S'POSE I'D BETTER. 'COS, AFTER ALL, FORE-WARNED IS FOREARMED, AND IF ANYTHING BAD IS GOING TO HAPPEN I MIGHT JUST AS WELL KNOW ABOUT IT!

TEE-HEE! NOTHING BAD'S GOING TO HAPPEN TO ME...

...BUT A DIRTY GREAT ROCK IS GOING TO DROP ON THAT WHISKERY OL' WIZARD'S BRAINLESS BONCE!

DEMON DRUID LIVES HERE — SO WATCH IT!

THIS I MUST SEE!

WHAT'S THIS I SEE? WIZARD PRANG ABOUT TO BE DIVE-BOMBED BY HIS OWN FOUL-FEATHERED ALLY?

I WOULDN'T HAVE MISSED THIS FOR ANYTHING!

CRRRUMP!

BOING!

EEK! HOW DID THAT HAPPEN?

SIMPLE, MY DOPEY DRUID! ENGELBERT AND I HAVE MERELY BEEN TESTING MY NEW INTERIOR-SPRUNG BONCE PROTECTOR!

CRRRUMP!

IF YOU MUST POKE YOUR NOSE INTO OTHER PEOPLE'S EXPERIMENTS, THEN YOU MUST EXPECT TO BECOME VICTIM OF A CERTAIN AMOUNT OF FALL-OUT!

AWRRRK!

GRRRRR!

ROTTEN, STUPID CRYSTAL BALLS! ALL THEY EVER GIVE ME IS DUFF INFORMATION... IT ISN'T EVEN AS IF I CAN GET TELEVISION PROGRAMMES ON THEM!

BIFF!

BASH!

KICK!

BOOF!

22

SCATTY BAT

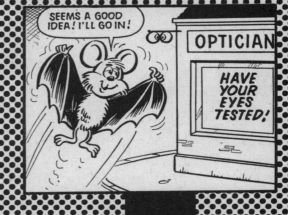

The SHIVER GIVERS

I'LL GATECRASH THIS PARTY AND EARN MYSELF A MILLION POUNDS INTO THE BARGAIN!

I'VE COME TO TRY FOR THE MILLION QUID!

BAH! YOU WOULD HAVE TO PICK TONIGHT!

WE'VE GOT A GATECRASHER AMONGST US...LET'S GET RID OF HIM QUICK, LADS!

CHEEK! I'LL SHIFT HIM, INNKEEPER!

BOO! WAIL! MOAN!

DO YOU CALL THAT HAUNTING? HUMPF!

YEEOW!

SQUEEEEEAK!

BONK!

28

YOU CAN BE IT! *TITTER!*

NO PEEPING NOW!

I WON'T! HEE, HEE!

BAH! YOU'RE CHEATING AGAIN... THERE'S NO-ONE ON THIS CHAIR!

THERE IS! *GIGGLE!*

YOU'RE SITTING ON ME!

YIKES! I'VE GONE RIGHT THROUGH HIM!

I'VE GOT TO THINK OF A WAY TO GET RID OF THIS JOKER... OF COURSE, *THAT'S IT!*

RIGHT! EVERYONE UP FOR A *CONGA!*

GREAT... MAKE A LINE BEHIND ME, FELLAHS!

WHAT'S THE INNKEEPER UP TO NOW?

STOP MAKING THOSE MINCED EYES FOR A MINUTE, COOKIE! I NEED YOUR HELP!

BAH! NOTHING BUT INTERRUPTIONS!

KITCHEN

ICING SUGAR

I HATE BILE

SHAM PAIN

30

33

GRIMLY FEENDISH

RUMBLE!
CLATTER!
KRASH!

GAAH! HOW CAN A MASTERMIND LIKE ME THINK UP NEW CRIMES WITH THAT ROW GOING ON?

IT'S THE *UNDERGROUND RAILWAY,* MR. FEENDISH! IT RUNS *NEAR* HERE!

IT DOES, EH? THIS GIVES ME A GREAT NEW FEENDISH IDEA!

START DIGGING, SQUELCH!

WHAAT?

LATER...

HEH, HEH! I'M GOING TO START A NEW UNDERGROUND LINE — *THE CROOKED LINE!* LEADING TO MY CELLAR!

HEY! *PINCHLEY CENTRAL?* I DON'T REMEMBER THIS STOP!

PINCHLEY CENTRAL

GASP! GRIMLY FEENDISH! PULL THE ALARM LEVER!

THAT'LL BE A TEN POUND FINE FOR IMPROPER USE, FOR A START!

ALARM LEVER

ALL MONEY MUST BE SHOWN AT THE BARRIER! THANK YOU, SAH!

GRR! I'M NOT PUTTING UP WITH THIS!

EXIT

£5

CHOC

IN THAT CASE I'LL HAVE TO PUT THE SQUEEZE ON!

OOOF!

SQUEEZE!

I'LL JUST CHECK EVERYONE'S PAID!

I'LL FIX HIM!

MIND THE DOORS!

ZONK!

THERE'LL BE A NICE UNDERGROUND CELL WAITING FOR YOU AT THE POLICE STATION, GRIMLY!

BAH! IT'S TUBE MUCH! I DRAW THE LINE AT THIS!

38

SHAKE

D

THE DESERT FOX

OOER! THE GERMAN GUARDS HAVE SPOTTED ME!

DER GRUB STORE

BUT THAT'S NO PROBLEM! I CAN BURROW MY WAY TO SAFETY! THEY CAN'T FOLLOW ME DOWN HERE!

WANT A BET, FOXY?

WHIRR!

YIKES! WH-WHAT IS IT?

DER "DESERT MOLE"! DER LATEST GERMAN SECRET WEAPON! IT CAN DER FOLLOW YOU ANYWHERE!

47

SHAKE

Sweeny Toddler

BUT, A LITTLE LATER...

WHAT ARE THOSE PEOPLE DOING IN THE GARDEN?

SOLD FOR FOURPENCE!

EEK! HE'S HOLDING AN AUCTION!

AND HERE'S YOUR VASE...OOER, MUM!

EEEK! MY VALUABLE ANTIQUE!

OH HERE, GO AND BUY SOME SWEETS OR I'LL NEVER GET DAD'S DINNER READY!

ME WON... ME WON!

WOOOPS!

SLIP!

CHINK!

YOU CAN'T CATCH ME AGAIN!

PHEW! YOU CAN SMELL THE ONION FROM HERE!

WAAAH! MY MONEY GONE DOWN DRAIN!

THAT ONION CAUSED REAL TEARS THIS TIME!

Mirth

Shakers

TOUGH NUTT and SOfty Centre

LOOK, SOFTY'S BUILT A SNOWMAN... LET'S BASH IT UP WITH SNOWBALLS!

HEY, SOFTY? DON'T YOU MIND US SMASHING DOWN YOUR SNOWMAN?

NOPE...!

GRR... THROW SNOWBALLS AT ME, EH?

...BUT I THINK TOUGH NUTT DOES! TEE, HEE!

G-GULP!

THAT'S GOT RID OF TOUGHY... I'LL BE SAFE FOR A WHILE NOW!

LATER...

THOSE KIDS SEEM TO BE HAVING FUN... I THINK I'LL JOIN 'EM!

MUM'S FUR COAT WILL KEEP ME WARM! TEE, HEE!

55

MEANWHILE, OUTSIDE...

ATTENTION! A BEAR HAS ESCAPED FROM THE ZOO...!

POLICE

GULP! I HOPE IT DOESN'T COME ROUND THIS WAY!

YIKES! IT'S THE ESCAPED BEAR!

PLEASE DON'T EAT ME, MR. BEAR ...PLEASE!

YOU DON'T HAVE TO BEG, OLD CHAP... I PROMISE I WON'T EAT YOU! HEE, HEE!

GRR! IT'S SOFTY! I'LL TEACH YOU TO MAKE A FOOL OUT OF ME!

I'M GOING TO GIVE YOU A GOOD PELTING!

NO, KEEP AWAY, YOU BRUTE!

HO, HO! SOFTY'S FOR IT NOW...!

SPORTS SCHOOL

SHAKE

63

THE DESERT FOX

THE DESERT WAR IN 1942...

HMM, A CAMP CONCERT! I WONDER IF I COULD USE THAT TO GRAB SOME GRUB?

CONCERT IN THE CANTEEN— TONIGHT

RIGHT, LET'S GO TO OUR TENTS AND REHEARSE FOR TONIGHT!

HEY! THAT GIVES ME AN IDEA!

I'LL AUDITION THEM ALL— STARTING WITH THE STAR!

STAR

♪ THERE'S A BOY COMING HOME ON LEAVE... ♫

SHE'S NO GOOD FOR MY PLAN— SHE'S TOO GOOD!

AT THE NEXT TENT...

BAH! THEY'RE NO GOOD EITHER— THE BOYS WILL LOVE 'EM!

moana lisa

MOAN! GRIPE! MOAN AND MORE MOANS!

ONE HOUR OF MOANING LATER...

I CAN'T STAND NO MORE! SOB! WAIL!

OH, DEAR! NOW IT'S A *CRYING* HYENA!

SERVES IT RIGHT!

AT THE ELEPHANT HOUSE...

TURN ROUND YOU GREAT FAT LUMP! I WANT TO SEE YOUR LONG NOSE!

CHEEKY BRAT...TAKE THAT!

GRR! I'VE HAD ENOUGH OF YOUR MOANING...YOU CAN STAY IN THERE NOW!

HEY!

WE'RE GOING TO SEE THE REST OF THE ZOO IN PEACE...WE'LL COME BACK FOR YOU LATER, MOANA!

WHAT'S THAT ANIMAL CALLED, MISTER?

THAT'S A *MOANA LISA GRIPER!* THEY'RE VERY RARE, THANK GOODNESS!

LOLLY POP

SPORTS SCHOOL

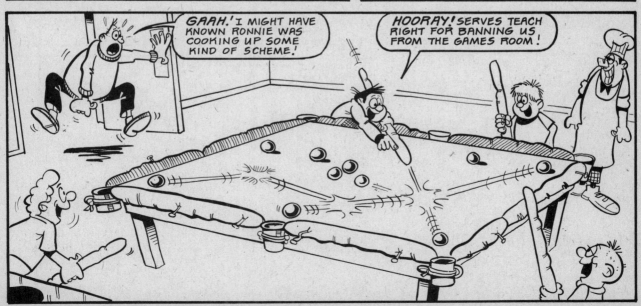

The FOREST LEGION

BECAUSE I'M HOLDING IT UP, THAT'S WHY! BUT... NOT FOR LONG!

..DOWN IT GOES ....THE WRONG WAY! *TIMBER!*

YUK YUK!

AAAGH! YOU DIM DUMMY, BUTCH! *ACROSS* THE ROAD I SAID ..NOT ON OUR *GETAWAY CAR!*

CRUNCH!

REALLY! *THAT SNAKE!* I NEEDN'T HAVE WASTED MY TIME PUNCTURING THE TYRES!

HISS

HISS

HISS HISS

I CAN SEE THE VAN COMING! QUICK, BUTCH! *PLAN 'B'!* LIE DOWN IN THE MIDDLE OF THE ROAD AND PRETEND YOU'VE HAD AN ACCIDENT! THE VAN WILL STOP...*THEN,* WE'LL KNOCK THE MEN OUT!

THE DESERT FOX

DISGRACEFUL—YOU LET THE *DESERT FOX* GET TO THE GRUB STORE! YOU'RE GOING TO BE STRIPPED OF YOUR UNIFORM, CORPORAL JONES!

OH, NO!

RIP!

IT WASN'T POOR, OLD JONES'S FAULT! I'M JUST TOO *SMART!*

IF ONLY THERE WAS SOME WAY I COULD HELP!

WAIT A MINUTE! I'VE GOT IT!

Blunder Puss

85

89

Shakers

ASTRO-NUT - he's out of this world!

WHAT MONSTER EARTHLINGS!

HO! HO! THEY'VE MADE SOME ROBOT MONSTERS! VERY CLEVER!

BUT *THEY* HAVEN'T ANY LIQUID TO SPLASH THEMSELVES WITH... I'LL GET THEM SOME!

HERE YOU ARE - SOME LIQUID!

NOW YOU CAN HAVE A GOOD SPLASH!

WHAT DID I DO WRONG?

FTOOM!

99

THE DESERT FOX

WE'VE BEEN CUT OFF FROM THE REST OF THE REGIMENT...IT'S *FIFTY MILES* TO OUR CAMP AND WE'VE NO *FOOD* OR *WATER!*

BOY! WAS I A MUG TO THINK I COULD SCROUNGE ANYTHING OFF THIS LOT?

PUFF! PANT!

PANT! LOOK, SIR! THE *VULTURES* ARE HOVERING OVERHEAD — WAITING FOR US..!

I'M AFRAID, CHAPS, IT LOOKS AS THOUGH WE'VE HAD OUR CHIPS! BUT STIFF UPPER LIP, WHAT!

HEY! LOOK AT THAT GREAT BIG WISH BONE!

HORRORNATION STREET

TUT, TUT! AFTER TWO THOUSAND YEARS, OUR HOUSES ARE IN A REAL MESS!

THERE'S NOTHING FOR IT... WE'LL HAVE TO STAY IN A HOTEL!

HOTEL

HOTEL de POSH

TOOT

HOTEL RECEPTION

WELCOME TO HOTEL DE POSH! IF YOU'LL SIGN THE REGISTER!

INK

The HAND

111

CREEPY CAR

HONEST HAROLD'S USED CARS

AH— THERE'S A NICE LOT OF CARS TO HIDE AMONGST!

I THINK I'LL BACK INTO THIS SPACE IN THE MIDDLE AND HAVE A LITTLE SNOOZE...

OH, MR. FIGLEY— THAT LOOKS LIKE A CUSTOMER!

YES, MR. HAROLD...

HE LOOKS LIKE A MUG— FLOG HIM THAT HEAP IN THE MIDDLE BEFORE IT FALLS TO BITS!

SO THAT'S THEIR LITTLE GAME!

AH! I CAN SEE YOU'RE AN **EXPERT**! JUST LISTEN TO THIS ENGINE— IT PURRS LIKE A KITTEN!

LOOKS NICE!

THIS CALLS FOR MY ANIMAL IMITATIONS!

MOOOOOOO CLUCK! BAAA! WOOF! WOOF! COCKADOODLE-DOO!

A KITTEN YOU SAID?

FRANKIE STEIN

ONE VERY COLD NIGHT—B-R-R-R!

CLATTER! CHATTER! CLACK!

IN THE NEXT BEDROOM...

I CAN'T SLEEP FOR ALL THAT NOISE COMIN' FROM FRANKIE'S BEDROOM. I'LL BE GLAD WHEN HE'S CHATTERED ALL HIS TEETH OUT!

CLATTER! CLACKITY-CLICK-CLICK-RATTLE!

A SLEEPLESS TWELVE HOURS LATER...

I'LL FIX HIM TONIGHT! THIS SPECIAL BUBBLY GUM I'M MAKING WILL MUFFLE HIS MOLARS!

GLUB! GLUE! BLUB!

COMES BED-TIME...

HERE'S SOMETHING FOR YOU TO CHEW IN BED, FRANKIE. IT'S CALLED "GUGGLY GUM".

OO! THANKS!

BUT...

GOO! THIS STUFF'S PLUGGED UP ME FANGS!

CHOMPH! GLOYSH! GLULCH! SPLODGE! GLULP!

AND IN DAD'S ROOM...

GLOYSH! SCHLUB! GLULCH! SQUIDGE!

ERK! IT SOUNDS LIKE AN OVER-LOADED TRIPE-SORTING MACHINE OPERATING IN A SEMOLINA PUDDIN'!

SO FORTY-EIGHT SLEEPLESS HOURS LATER...

HUH! I'LL SILENCE THEM CLASHIN' GNASHERS TONIGHT!

HELLO, RUBBER COMPANY—AH—SEND ME A ROLL O' RUBBER SHEETIN' RIGHT AWAY!

THROB! ICE

AND AT BED-TIME, AFTER HALF A DAY'S WORK IN THE LAB...

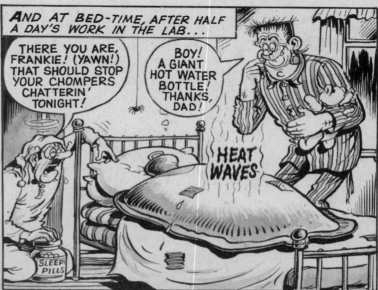

THERE YOU ARE, FRANKIE! (YAWN!) THAT SHOULD STOP YOUR CHOMPERS CHATTERIN' TONIGHT!

BOY! A GIANT HOT WATER BOTTLE! THANKS, DAD!

HEAT WAVES

SLEEP PILLS

ONE GHASTLY SECOND LATER — IN FRANKIE'S ROOM...

DREAM-LAND! — 'ERE WE COME —!! ERK!

CRASH!

WHOOSSH!

ZIP!

POP!

POYN-NG!

THE BED'S COLLAPSIN'!

BAH! NOW I'LL BE COLD AGAIN.

SLEWSH!

MEANWHILE, DAD HAD CURED HIS SLEEPING PROBLEM THROUGH EXHAUSTION...

—CLATTER-CLICK-CHATTER-RATTLE-CLICK-CLACK-KLAKITY!

Z-Z-Z-Z-Z-Z

...AND AT 6 A.M., HE'S UP FOR HIS USUAL BRISK WALK ROUND THE GARDEN BEFORE BREAKFAST...

A GREAT NIGHT'S SLEEP! THAT GIANT HOT WATER BOTTLE I MADE FOR FRANKIE CERTAINLY DID THE TRICK!

WHEN FRANKIE AND MICKY SEE THE CHANGE IN ME, THEY'LL THINK THEY'RE SEEING TH... AAAGH!?!

SKID!

WHOOSH!

HOT WATER — FROZEN SOLID!

CRASH!

SHATTER!

TINKLE!

SIX HOURS LATER, WHEN FRANKIE WOKE FOR HIS LUNCH...

WHAT'S HAPPENED? I MUST BE SEEIN' THINGS — OR IS IT DAD?

EXOTIC BLOOMS UNDER CULTIVATION. KEEP DOOR CLOSED.

BLAH-H!

28 SLEEPLESS NIGHTS LATER, IN THE MEN'S WARD OF THE PUDDLEDITCH INFIRMARY...

STOP 'EM! GAG 'EM! GIMME EARPLUGS! IT'S DRIVIN' ME MAD! HAH-HAH! AGH-H! MAD! LET ME GO HOME TO FRANKIE'S CHATTERIN' CHOMPERS!

STOP THAT GIBBERING THIS INSTANT, YOU SELFISH OLD BRUTE! YOU'LL WAKEN THE OTHER PATIENTS!

SNORE

Z-Z-Z

SNORT!

Z-Z-Z

KA-A-AK!

SNORE!

Z-Z-Z

KAW-WK

Z-Z-Z

SN

120

WE ARE! GULP!

HOW AM I GOING TO GET OUT? I WILL NEVER MAKE IT THROUGH THE DEEP SNOWDRIFTS!

BUT SHIVER CAN! GHOSTS CAN GO THROUGH ANYTHING!

YES, GRIMES?

SHIVER, YOU LOVABLE OLD GHOST, YOU — HAVE ALL THIS GRUB, ANYTHING... IF YOU'LL JUST GET THROUGH THE SNOW TO CIVILISATION AND BRING BACK HELP!

IT'S A DEAL!

SLURP!

I'LL BE OFF NOW, GRIMES!

THANKS, SHIVER, I WON'T FORGET THIS, AND—ERK! WHERE'S ALL THE SNOW GONE?

LATER...

GRRR! I'LL TEACH YOU TO GIVE AWAY ALL THE FOOD IN MY LARDER, YOU BARMY BUTLER!

WHAT WAS THAT GRIMES SAID ABOUT NEVER GIVING ME ANY FOOD? LOOKS LIKE HE'S HAVING TO EAT HIS WORDS!

GRIMLY FEENDISH

THE ROTTENEST CROOK in the WORLD!

The GHOST'S REVENGE

Scatty BAT

THAT SOPPY ARTIST HASN'T DRAWN A PLACE FOR ME TO HANG ON!

GLOOP! I HATE RAIN! I MUST TAKE COVER!

SO I'LL HANG ON TO THE FRAME!

AH! NICE AND DRY!

CREAK! SNAP!

OOPS! I SPOKE TOO SOON!

OUCH!

TRUST IDIOT ME TO HANG FROM A SLIDE TROMBONE!

The Duke's SPOOK

HEE, HEE! LOOK AT OLD GRIMESY TRAINING FOR THE FOOTBALL MATCH THIS AFTERNOON! HE'S PLAYING IN GOAL FOR THE DUKE'S TEAM!

PUFF! GRUNT!

EEEK! LET GO!

GRR! LAUGH AT ME, WOULD YOU? COME HERE!

AAH! THAT'S BETTER! JUST WHAT I NEED TO TOWEL MYSELF DOWN!

OOAARGH! STOPPIT!

HO, HO! THAT'LL TEACH HIM!

OOH! I FEEL ALL CRUSHED! BUT I'LL MAKE HIM SORRY!

THE MATCH STARTED...

I'LL PASS BACK TO GRIMES...!

GRIMLY FEENDISH

GRIMLY IS "INSIDE" AGAIN!

MOAN! MOAN!

IT'S MR. FEENDISH'S BIRTHDAY! I'VE BROUGHT HIM A CAKE!

H'MM!

COR!

JUST A MINUTE, GRIMLY—THIS CAKE LOOKS SUSPICIOUS!

HUH! AS I THOUGHT—A HIDDEN FILE! THAT'S AN OLD TRICK, GRIMLY!

BLUSH!

SIGH! WHAT'S THIS? A ROPE LADDER, DISGUISED AS ICING! TYPICAL! TYPICAL!

STIFLED YAWN!

HORRORNATION STREET

135

SKREEEK!

HEY, LADS! THERE'S SOMETHING ABOUT THAT CHAP IN THIS OLD BOOK OF MINE!

H-HE'S THE P-P-PHANTOM F-F-FIDDLER!

GULP!

A PHANTOM!

HE'S COME TO HAUNT US!

CACKLE!

GALLOP! GALLOP! GALLOP! GALLOP!

WAIT A MINUTE! WAIT A MINUTE!

WE'RE NOT GOING TO LET ANY PHANTOM SCARE US, ARE WE? IT'S US WHO ARE MEANT TO FRIGHTEN PEOPLE AROUND HERE!

ALL VERY WELL, BUT WHAT'S THE ANSWER TO HIM?

SQUEEL! WAIL!

WELL, YOU KNOW WHAT THEY SAY, DAD— IF YOU CAN'T BEAT 'EM...

TWAAAAANG! CLAAANG! WHINE!

SHRIEK! I HATES M-MODERN MUSIC!

...JOIN 'EM!

140

141

frankie stein's
A-MAZE-ING BRAIN

R.T.NIXON

IN HERE →

OUT HERE →

Professor Cube insists that everything he tells Frankie goes in one ear and out the other. Trace carefully through Frankie's brain and you will see that the Prof. is right!

142